In the Pure Block of the Whole Imaginary

In the Pure Block of the Whole Imaginary

Richard Meier

OMNIDAWN PUBLISHING
RICHMOND, CALIFORNIA
2012

Cover art by Jane Williams, photograph:
"East Boston, November 9, 2011"

Book cover and interior design by Cassandra Smith

Omnidawn Publishing is committed to preserving ancient forests and natural resources. We elected to print this title on 30% postconsumer recycled paper, processed chlorine-free. As a result, for this printing, we have saved:

2 Trees (40' tall and 6-8" diameter)
860 Gallons of Wastewater
1 million BTUs of Total Energy
54 Pounds of Solid Waste
191 Pounds of Greenhouse Gases

Omnidawn Publishing made this paper choice because our printer, Thomson-Shore, Inc., is a member of Green Press Initiative, a nonprofit program dedicated to supporting authors, publishers, and suppliers in their efforts to reduce their use of fiber obtained from endangered forests.

For more information, visit www.greenpressinitiative.org

Environmental impact estimates were made using the Environmental Defense Paper Calculator. For more information visit: www.edf.org/papercalculator

Library of Congress Cataloging-in-Publication Data

Meier, Richard, 1966-
    In the pure block of the whole imaginary / Richard Meier.
        p. cm.
    ISBN 978-1-890650-69-8 (pbk. : alk. paper)
    I. Title.
    PS3563.E3459I5 2012
    811'.54--dc23

                        2012014452

Published by Omnidawn Publishing, Richmond, California
    www.omnidawn.com   (510) 237-5472   (800) 792-4957
            10 9 8 7 6 5 4 3 2 1
            ISBN: 978-1-890650-69-8

Grateful acknowledgement is here made to my editor Rusty Morrison for the exemplary care and intelligence she brought to her reading and editing of this book.

And to Lisa Fishman, my reader.

And to James Fishman-Morren, beloved interlocutor.

Thanks to the editors of the following publications in which some of these poems have appeared, sometimes in different form: *Omnidawn poetry feature, Mrs. Maybe, with+stand, 1913: a journal of forms, h_ngm_n, Tammy, Letterbox, Mary: A Journal, Rabbit Light Video Magazine, Sorry for Snake,* and *MiPOesias*

Content

Afterword

A negative construct —
When a man can
sing — Each little bird
sings — Brothers in a
previous life — More
or less — The patience
of the trees — One day
a long detour —The
mason dumps — The
dissatisfied couldn't stand

A negative construct, the tree in the sun through a tree, the building in *they built the building for its space*, the space we can still see before exterior walls and windows and a roof. Is it a building yet, steel-forms, concrete, span, and how unlike the human body is this building built at its final scale, adding layers or being layers, the bricklayer with a t-shirt bandanaed around his nose and mouth, the bricklayer below the sky-isn't-blue-above-this-blue tarp, growth rings of plans and colors. Image of a microscopic building set among life (the book of common flowers with its names and full-page plates) and detritus — mineral, organic, once manufactured — of a wasteland, gestating. At what point in the building is space enviable? Union stickers on a construction helmet (yellow) hanging from a young woman's backpack. Clothes are constructed from pieces, after the gestation of elements — silk, oil, cotton; we were injected into a mold that can be removed and outlasts what it's shaping, unlike the wax that makes a single ring with figures out of its own disappearance, nothing created or destroyed but lasts in other forms. Dreams, coral, laws, rock walls, rules, handclaps accumulate.

When a man can sing and he is singing what I am thinking is how he can be singing here. The meadow without line breaks at the level of crickets, clover, electric guitar, and stopped singing to say there are lots of free things in summer and she was going to be all of them, in the desire to sleep *en plein aire*, like a first view of the Impressionist masterwork, face down in the entire field at once, collapsing westward in that flora till the night bugs woke, then fled, generation from its jokes; it's the placelessness the child mimics, pretending to pluck each poem from the grass before inventing all the things I did in the city and all the things I write and t f o z spells no stopping and no ambulance coming to the city. The trees hang down like monkeys the die cast.

Sitting on the sidewalk to lean against the parkfence, togetherness concepts are marsh grasses and a lady's hat in springtime, or the missing visitor list, lost or never filled out, names and numbers in held property, "until future release," as they refused to tell, your brother in his cell. On the phone the way home told that poem, e i, e i, o all that happened, all that wrote.

Each little bird sings in the flashlight. The nice bee makes honey. Kids transcribe the words of the dead in that precinct. A correspondence. Sails disappear without a horizon, in other words, as the literature of modernity pre-figured in the style-dependent philosophies and correspondences ultimately read without footnotes as the elusive space made by a movement. On the third deep breath he was sleeping. After it happened you didn't have to prepare for it, the summer green glimpsed through a window with its intense yellows and the garish pure green of your own cottage. Each little bird that sings sings in the flashlight finally, *Pendant quinze jours je m'étais confiné dans ma chambre, je m'étais entouré des livres à la mode dans ce temps-là* off a teleprompter, that glass book through which the faces of the audience are visible, standing and falling for a seat at the crumbling façades and unused chimneys. Meanwhile the untutored child (no longer a kid) types the words of the deaf, which only he hears clearly, back to them. He was like that, people said, whether that was like him or not. I saw him get off the bus. Oh ugly time — and space! His transfer had expired. I offered him a jam of chestnuts and clementines, another final *espacer*.

Brothers in a previous life? But if we took everyone's thoughts seriously, how many more would be sentenced to die? Coming out of an interior room into the miracle of weather, the pair of hands in the fountain turned into an eagle, disabusing us of the variable rewards in a handful (how natural the word seems) of clouds marking their own edges and the sun's. To wear the year's clothing all at once, might that satisfy the truth? It walked by without looking at us, and I'm afraid *the* is the appropriate word, however hard to say it the same way twice.

Death was general over all the provinces, and he could feel her feeling this to be part of her condition, cold and terrible and full of belonging, and in his excitement let her sleep while he rehearsed melodies from earlier in the conflict, before they'd found their way out to the place where the map had forced them in. What they'd done (the brothers) was slaughter a pig, poorly, until ongoingness appeared merciful. But part of a fantasy is better than one more complete, "all-consuming" as the indices New York, Tokyo, Caracas, Trieste, and the whole rest of the range that has come among us to be known as the midlands, the place where things happen at something so like their own pace. Into the pot of all successive seas, the sun dipped like a ladle.

More or less mechanically, the pink between the buildings and heads of
the passengers absorbed, radiated, and returned the feeling of walking
through a door into the room one was just leaving as the distance
between cities, two backyards and an alley. What promise did the day
hold? The unpremeditated mention of a name, the turgid folds. Where
two or more streets came together, thousands marched into that life. I
was a sentry of clouds once. Now the letter A, a black-skirted neighbor,
ascends 7 stairs after tipping a shopping bag of garbage in the bin. An
automatic garage door welds in white facets the sunflash to uneven bricks,
but only in succession; the light's completely gone when it's retracted.
If the attempt to step outside of working hours without stumbling
across one thing after another leaves us in omnipresence (lost inside and
outside), a stinky gray cloud, self-deflecting architecture of gas, then
stumbling itself, the little death of (just!) walking beside, counts the green
leaves in November's bare ruined crowns in the sound — scuffle and
scratch — revealing something, the death of the subject, squeezing you so
tightly to its side.

The patience of the trees or the patience in the man who grows them
— vivacious abominations, how superb to say there is a third possibility.
To say there is a third possibility going out and never coming back
while staying home and never leaving out. Nothing says, in the grid of
associations' dark wood of roots and swaled flowers in the meadow, or
in the grammar grid I see in the filigreed moon, with airplanes in the
role of denial of the thread and grain, that they are mornings that come
after naps called evenings, the lake darkening the relaxation of hard labor,
a black chiffon dress on the assembly line lowered, like a sunrise, over
rattlesnakes, irrigation tunnels, illegal imprisonment on the road that
led to the station wagon, its backwards face facing the criminal route
through the desert/mountains. Every room has a ceiling if only to stand
up and bang someone's head on it, dazed and happy, freed by that sky
of the remote possibility of evening's barbaric safety-net, yet sandy and
wireless. But the orders had stayed with us, even carried us, and we rolled
in the grass "above" the lake as if it were the mother of all free time. In
the allegory of the graph on graph paper, now stooped inside the mine,
now hunched and awkward as a low truck, now a splintered movement
in the Open Air, we were glowing with delight. A rebuke in the form of
a continuance, a continuance in the rebuke slammed into not to miss the
plot whose form we filled, squeezing into the wood full of spaces as it
was dark, grateful it seemed to us in the grass, our narrow freedom to be
touched, giving up the movement of the world in rift, clouds misnamed
as cloak or veil, far at last from the secret of things.

One day a long detour (around a collapsed bridge) led to the new look
of the hills, tilting like a teacup in the altered seat. A giant wooden sign's
(though smaller than the ones that emerged above the trees beside the
thruway) unequal legs sank visibly in the hillside, advertising a motel,
Whispering Pines, made of the same substance as the name and the sign.
Fate and chance lived in three places at once I walked through and into
and never shook off, a fine coating of silt in whose grit and topography
I spied the content — its feeling in my shape — where I had expected
to see the texture of what I naively called the figure in the langscape, a
misunderstanding she'd made up, having once seen a man chest deep
in the lake trying to make a space around himself. His whole life was a
resistance and a fight. But this was one of his moments of emergence and
of a new splendor. Long notes of a French horn from the building three
doors down felt a peculiar surging joy. The marks I'd made in the sand
on the floor of the cell showed it to be my own, as the nanny pointed
out, while the lover of images refused to look, though she would have
welcomed his body in the novel which to him it seemed already to have
entered, as the names in his cellphone had been replaced, in the dream,
before he'd ever had one, by those of people he'd known inside those
buildings. Where would it have been? she said, if the resistance had been
ours.

The mason dumps his bucket on the beach then thrashes his shirt against a tree, breasts bouncing. A partner leans below the old Voyager or Caravan and checks the oil. The dust from the building joins the leaves in a spiral. The seasons will not be reversed; a gull's feather crosses the sand. I'm not talking about you, but the guys who work with you, the super shouts. The shoulders of the beer drinkers touch, the bench softens, contrails cross, a dog grinds out its howls on the bricks, and the super seeks in vain to reconnect a single worker to a single action. How angry one must get to describe a response. And the drunks on the pier plant their chair and shout to Joy, Are you with us? as she hugs one of another two on a shoreline bench, threatening to swallow us all like the clouds being blown over a horizon. I always help everyone, her loud complaint in the shade of oaks, soon to be overtaken by the shade of bricks.

The dissatisfied couldn't stand side-by-side, but slid apart together, a strand of glass on which we glided further and further up, pulled through figures we cut in the ice — the 8, the 0 and the *whip*. A world of spinning cliffs began the moment we halted.

Now the red-throated are shaking the fullness of space from the once-green branches, the old hallucination replaced by an equality of the leaf, in whose recursions the face appears in unseeable lengths of fiber, spanning sibilants whose giant sound (the sand has become a snake) give mountains and megaplexes the appearance of lost loved ones finally found.

Snow falls. I walk the perimeter of a stranger's yard, wretched monster, making each flora and fauna track the sun, fearing that these chiaroscuros end.

They actually had —
The happiness of —
Things that move —
Boxes put away — The
child thought —
Walking home — The
clearest image —
Smallest degraded
figure

They actually had seemed like repetitive physical actions when I met them coming down the street, each of us in one of those pools of light that show by their ragged edges the nature of the place entered. When they passed, as a valley describes the water in land, though none of it remains, first or individual impressions followed to my strangely moving feet, whose motions were as sweeping and divorced, from what I knew and where I went, as the arc of headlights crossing the ceiling above me as I lie in bed are from the cars passing muffled by the night breeze through the street. And how much more so from the figure in the bed, so little was their motion mine, so vividly perceived, including the space between, in which the facets of the flat sidewalk shone, split, and bubbled, and the black strip between quivering autumn leaves, moment by moment, gave way or invaded. Everything was OK only in that sense of a timeless neither-for-nor-againstness cradled, or was it cabled, by the spinning, yellow from the front, the rear and the sides. Is non-action truly the greater of the two, admiring the contempt in the boys' contraposto as they note in passing the demonic police car? And do you think the essences differ, she added, chin nearing her shoulder, and when we leave, the shadow will remain here with them? A t-shirt to change into at the entrance to the center had put asunder the signs and colors in favor of a change in signs and colors, the signs and colors of the place come into, a change in ownership that ceases to know us, and by which we must, in those parts and these, be known.

The happiness of the group has always been revealed in its exclusion of you, the only individual in the room, to whom even I, your creator, won't deign to speak. In response, the lonely interlocutor made a sweater out of a cotton ball, and pinned it to the bulletin board, where it has begun to resemble a cloud through which the moon shines, in the form of the marbled orb that was made to harden around the buried pin holding in place, as you had long suspected, that which, but for this function, would have obscured it. To this we have consigned that still small and unsigned voice, whom we answer as and play so lightly, with such pleasure, in the privacy of our room, where the bulletins, like the little strip of lake visible from one corner of the bed, which is itself visible from the desk, have been issued from the right hand to the left, the one in the pocket of Nadar's Baudelaire below Greff's hand-tinted *Louvre*, and the one in the loom where Ariadne spins her songs, and is it only by that conscription (yes) we can be here. There is no season longer than the summer, while you weep among the crowd of pleasure-seekers, though we, in this Plutonic dialogue, move along.

Things that move through space include words. A calculus. I know where you are but you can't be reached. Things follow like shadows in the shadow of the hand when the light is from the right, from the morning, from the lake, as later they will, still above the orange velvet of the chair, chase the same sad *how* without fear of catching or hope of being caught. What are you thinking? I fall, I find it in memory. By a thunderclap I am awake. The system I imagined brings tears to my eyes by its existence in the shade we walked on, that sat up suddenly and began to speak. The inability to live without any one of you three little pigs, city bridge, triangle of children in the crabgrass running, having forgotten motion, led me to the thicket of questions through the small picket line at the Hotel Congress and onto that shining path the urge to follow can eye for a while without sinking, through sails and breakwaters to the undulating horizon of fire and water describing neither the house of mourning nor the house of mirth but the first time what you had written turned against you and convinced you that you were with it, opposite figure, your ancient double poking through the bins, briefly ahead of you on the shifting path, on which the only order is, turn back, turn back, as the sound of drums in the public park multiplies the crowd of sails into a din, and again I doubted *within*.

Boxes put away, room for the clouds, which had they gone to school
would perhaps never have existed. A brilliant pink line above the four-
flats suggested another life, less productive, free of benefit, but still
preferable, like a golf club on a garage roof and Montaigne's discarded
essays. He says, Great souls go much further; they give us examples of
escapes that are not only steady and composed, but even proud. And still
the unlived life, after contemplation filled some others with dismay, and
though he himself, armed with dull powers of apprehension, persisted
in imagining a country in which the clouds' changed colors, now livid
as grapes in the Concord belt, took up a cause outside provenance. An
airplane whistled like the sea but receded. We appeared, among old
identity card photos, to do the same, as clouds and resistance did. In a
nest cloaked with old, peaceful words, mouse dumped from the desk
drawer into long grass from which it would return, I forgot fall colors,
no art being an ascension in itself of hills that lead to fortified villages. A
description of a street walked down, finding the very thing needed, still
appears in a book written before it.

The child thought it strange to define words with other words. What did you draw? The man thought he was looking at a purple oval with a touch of yellow. I drew that, the child answered ecstatically, feeling the paper with his finger. The frost is a little behind the shadows. A slash of tree trunk and the L of the roof. We hate a work of art that finds designs inside us, better to lie in the fog of melting snow and see the lake that remains and the person who has left, the ones we would rather not see but do in this reduction. What I loved about the little box full of *hair elastics* and *bobby pins* was my own wonder at the little squares of wood, 6 to a side, each of which had its own cross-section of branch, as if it had found something that could be wholly repeated when dispersed. The child, between the toilet and the window, liked the way it opened and spilled the many-colored elastics. An after-image of the monks spot-welding an iron fence in orange robes at night while we drove past fell apart in the nest of elastics, blue and orange among them. The ruins of December are full of people. Feeling is lost. The melted lake, re-frozen, clear as a picture plane in the public park, drags in its current a bit of duckweed torn at the root, bright-green, but it stops when the skater does and reveals its stasis. Further out, a void that can be seen clearly through this fiction starts the world in orbit around involuted space. Participation is voluntary as the wind pushes a glove and a cry faster through the deeps of sky and cloud than the ear and hand that released them. Now that the ocean is gone I am sail and ship, but the embargo on motion means he can only be thrown away, the hour you were queen. Go to work we tell the child. Go to work, go to work, go to work.

Walking home from the elevated train that by our stop (Rockwell) had reached, like a chart of the working day, ground level, the man without a dog said have you seen my dog and I knew I hadn't. He greeted me with a hand on the fence that separated us both from the parking lot and the direction in which he'd spoken; he was speaking to that explosion of space that had overwhelmed us, to my left and his right as we passed in opposite directions, in the sense that his dog was lost in the sense that he didn't have one. It's the lack of total domination that holds us in the sway of these utopian gestures. While the magic triad darkened in the veins of Madame Bovary, the collective dandy shone from its thousand algorithmic windows, behind which its constituents labored for the rooms in the clouds they already occupied. Outlined on the glass phallus in which one (I am part of them) was high enough to hear the sirens and not respond with purple-blue, pink, light-blue, they saw themselves imprinted on the age. By a fragment the dandy meant a building or two, not part of a sentence. Yet the effort not to take a position — which I mean in the only, the military, sense — ate at the heart of how I stood, thinking of willow trees by the river, telling the tale of our construction with the failure to stand absolutely as the orange light glided up those structures, lot and tower, toward a parting I was attempting to name a network to set against the network.

The clearest image of this phenomenon: a man is walking on the embankment between Highway 11 and a soybean field, between Highway 11 and a meadow, between Highway 11 and the small pines growing in the waste ground behind the local high school athletic field. Beside him is always a fence, a deer fence, a highway fence, a chain-link fence, a barbed-wire fence. (*What is the law? Is the law a fence?*) The grass on the top of the embankment is mowed down (the cross-country team races along this embankment and sometimes there are white arrows painted in the grass, showing the way) and on the side of the embankment it grows up, along with sumac, phlox, foxtail, and the rest. The wind is with him or against him or to one side or absent, allowing the bugs to stay or driving them away. Sun or clouds or parts of each. And at a certain point, beside the deer fence or above a passing truck or halfway past the soy field, he knows he is going to turn around, or keep going, but before he turns around, or after he has turned but before he turns again and keeps going, he is in two places at once and in the time it takes to color his being, one of those white carnations whose freshly-cut stem has been set in a vase of colored liquid, but before the future has reached the petals, the creepy feeling, of things, people, ideas and events one has been told will cease to matter so terribly in the future ceasing to matter before the future has arrived, has tainted both directions, the words gradually filling in their referents. What a useless short-term prophecy, the one that appears as sickening inversion — walking forwards, I am walking backwards; having turned for home, I am setting out again — in the stomach, lightening in the head, clarity of leaves bunched on a spring tree or clinging to one in fall in the eyes, sun collecting in a single brilliant spot on the seemingly flat surface in one after another of the automobiles. But then one realizes, while one is often sad and often angry, one is always happy, content, without even the desire, which the teacher has, not to know what that word means.

Smallest degraded figure: with the hip of snow and the flowery black peaks against the sky. All horizons are the funeral island, Lawrence, Byron. Walking away from the wet-green-paint kitchen of Apartment Living to the path by the river of No Human Contact, palazzo of huge emission pipes elbowed down into the canal, Department of Water, sunlight jittering inside the shadowy arcade. A keen bright upward feeling of falling down the steep slope to the town and the beasts and the people. The dimmest, most mature vision the sand mapped out in dolly tracks froze as the face was imagined having to touch that window with its hands. The mask of a door or letter — one feels through it — that it isn't a mask — the black helmet under the arm of the meter reader in from his motorcycle — a doorbell heard for the first time — though one might have kept sleeping — nothing to be removed or recognized.

She might! and what then? — Forward and back — The frame of the locked — Akin to not having — But here were these buildings — I knew

She might! And what then? The Imperial road! The south? Italy? What then? Was it a way out? It was only a way in again. It came near the end. Was the old idea helpful, that new ideas are hard to understand only because they are unfamiliar, quoting Rimbaud in a police station without knowing it? The sound of the keys makes the keys crash into the form and its carbons and tells (but who?) that you are again where you are, so far from that perspective that had first attracted you to the slow and historical process of becoming just that. Then the child asked if it was morning, because he had woken in the light of afternoon. Dresden was not London, Paris or what was coming, but the slow seeping awareness in the wrists a thudding loosened pulse. The brilliant color of an old Polaroid against the windowsill, thunk of the mechanism when it came out, counting and twitching of the wrist. Was it in him, this thing he had conjured, or was he now stuck, free to look at and serve it, still in the imperially open space, a lake of slush at the corner of Lawrence St. and Western Ave., near Lincoln Square, Chicago, Illinois? A door into a room, a woman in black runs through a gate, the record shop where Anna works has a window. But there is that other kind too, plucked from the roadside, mingled with the great forces' coins in her purse/your pocket. Cough cough — *poor little thing* precedes the feeling — *Stay* — Nana comes running.

Forward and back, the center held in reserve, passed through on the way to the ends that each necessitated a return. A field clear-cut but for a few trees or a few trees to a meadow allowed to return and beyond that the lake shore a boy on the ice had pronounced the edge of the sea, not sure. Not married, dreaming of divorce, a manager with no workers, a worker with a distant boss who didn't know your face, a knowledge that could be avoided — it had been given to you as advice — for years, a blue spot with a white center too bright to see. Invisibility is another way to be absorbed. There's a spot where the ice is no longer over the sand and the waves have hollowed it out from beneath. The soldier in his camouflage is more visible than anyone on the train. Shapes cut from a transparent sheet on which the light stretches and bends cover his hands, trees rimed with ice, shapes repeating repeat. Three men shoveling snow make the letters of the letter-writer's name, doubled over, flinging, at rest.

The frame of the locked bike is missing a tire, handlebars and a seat. I
would like to be seen, but not as I am. Covered Wood he always heard
when the station was announced when the poem was full of writing, not
receding from its subject, but being written inside it, until he stopped
at an ice-gray desk and at last saw the sparks from the express light up
the walls, recognizing his own motion revolving in its sudden stillness
as the frames and passengers flashed past. And there must be a point in
the middle *into* becomes *out from* but perhaps never a time when *through*
becomes *beyond*, a value in the painting of gold and lapis lazuli and
another one where the train plunges through the snow and the whipped,
unaltered snow falls behind. The poet-passenger falling almost asleep
inside the sound of his fellow travelers frees the train from the glare
of the snow to be reflected in a long stretch of abandoned warehouses,
undifferentiated dark stretches of busted out windows, coo-roo of
pigeons, and white-washed graffiti, until it sinks gradually into a culvert
where two exit and ascend a staircase to the station and the surface, to
which the engine and passengers make no more claim than to a cloud.
Those two — one seems almost to lead and the other almost to follow —
will find the town green covered up, and visit for a while before passing
away. Today the icy sidewalk sends a dozen stabilizing muscles to work at
every step, while the flat light brightens at last in the early evening as the
street lights return and divide from the crystallized objects, stick, fence
post, plastic bag, umbrella.

Akin to not having been there at the worst moment (a birth) and then returning to address it, from a yet greater distance, as one of the things of the class seen *entirely*, also having joined it, as if the tree in the hay field looked askance at the approaching figure squinting and tilting, an actor trying to see through the mask he'd been given, that was pressed on him, the inverted side, the side without paint, a god invented so he might look out. People in love are sometimes not loving anyone. Your stockinged foot left the room like the crow's shadow that crossed the notionally Buddhist garden, illuminating the thin red flowers of the moss sitting on the bricks followed by the sound of its voice, as the book of love sometimes was/is followed by the book of anger. Every trip to the right margin is a little incursion into the spectacle, a day trip which included a viciously automatic return. Maybe I need to change it to crook of love and crook of anger to sound your concern about sound and imitation, the picture of the spring lamb in the crook of the man's arm who promised to kill and eat it. Sleeping on the floor knees and elbows and wrists went numb, fell asleep, developed an aversion to control. Keys, bobby pins, pennies, license: what do you have in common? The plop of coffee into milk, the image of fire projected on the back of the space heater, the breath with which you intermittently sleep, and how does one see anything besides the regularity of the letters? As if the rows themselves were sown and reaped, cut open and wept.

But here were these buildings moving under leaf-shadow, backs to the
river and ass to the rubble. Parturition. The radiators hissed. I described
two figures in the clouds, side by side, triangular heads, as you refused
an erotics that included images, the traditional home-made newsstand
(soon to be replaced by design-standards) of corrugated steel and two-
by-fours staring at pornography. The finger-blackened coin of the moon
hung above the Ferris wheel like an account of our passage into the hell
of beautiful things while we searched for the dispersing hammer in desire
that would annihilate that self unsure until we asked was the flower male
or female and felt in one crevice after another its collection. But why be
anti- anything? Barbed wire connects these divided countries, links the
continents to the islands, and "the Babylon of scented gardens" (by which
we recognized the morgue) is very close. It's written in ash, more than
six hundred thousand pieces. You think that you are present at the very
creation of the world.

"I knew he was going to end up in jail." But I knew the jail surrounded by a meadow, motorcycles and cars lined up outside apartments, where doing nothing (three ponds and a bay within the realm of freedom) had expanded long since beyond recognition our repetitive physical actions. Returned by a stranger, every thought swims into and then out of focus, in the book being read. Corn and wheat are grown by prisoners at the farm — rows and bars shine — but a ridge of numerous narrow strips contains no certainty but greater and lesser. There aren't any false feelings we might reconcile.

Nobody bought — A little cottage — From the dinner table — Where, by such and such — These people, that tower — The sight of wind — Only no one wants — Supreme circumstance

Nobody bought the new century, and having left that soon-to-be-demolished aperitif, 2nd-hand view of vigilante roomettes, I traced the outrage of face value in a book from two black eyeholes, as the child described you on the other side of the curtsy, attempting to find whether the attempt to find a style appropriate to all circumstances was beyond the good and evil (a fence of spaces, totally clear, are posted between each frame) of things and names, names that are also business to thousands, whom we never meet, though we are among us in their presence, except the odd power (girl) drawing forms (flowers) on the rhetoric (sidewalk) in the time (chalk) amidst the first terrorism (raindrops). It (she) greeted me once then reappeared constantly in my narrow language (precincts, conscription). Nevertheless I continued to recognize it (her) from television (antecedents), when considered a sin, as Flaubert said, the most bourgeois among them.

A little cottage by the sea, a cottage of flowers, *Casina de Fiori*, with a bell and a lemon tree and a view of the sea, a great V ending in immersion beginning a loss of self that returned and began again those long afternoons when the heat seemed to prevent more and more from going out so less and less returned, a fine pulse that could have belonged to either of anyone. A man on the beach inside a rack of brightly colored skirts moved in little jumps and kicks as if propelled by a shrugging of the Earth. Trojan work. Bites of the sea inside a peach grew larger, glazing the day until it fell asleep beside them. But a general explanation pinned us to the mountain. We saw the heatwave on the coast, penciled numbers in an herbarium diary requiring the thought that nothing anymore belonged to anyone. Clouds of gnats beside the brook, an image that was the limit of what?

From the dinner table we looked out over the newspaper and oranges into a house where trees with jug handle trunks dressed the flanks of a black mountain that balanced on its struts the red sun. We felt we belonged here. The smudged hands on the table were ours, having just dropped the paper, and the tunic's red and blue stripes belonged to the sky, but whomever's house we looked out into shared a roofline with the ridge the planes flew lower than. We forbid ourselves to lift our eyes to the ceiling above our solitary table. What if everything that had ever happened wasn't there? A country surrounded us, more countries, a sea, a strait, a gulf, an ocean. The 24 time zones of every hour cast so many shadows the oranges sat off-center in a gray halo and the red blur, having outstripped the sound of its engine, struggled not to move past the beaver's dark fur or the rabbit's patchwork field, perched on the head of the woman in the house. The crowd roared across the wall. A State Highway Department Fence in the median prevented crossing over. It was all coming back. A cannonball fired into the interior was likely to strike an Indian, we opened the door and went into the mountain.

Where, by such and such a number, on the slovenly grid, sensation become imaginary, lacking putative edges, in one of those gaps where space is infinite, the lake's pure razor-mussel blue has been forced into sky, wall, and/or proximate, fast-approaching horizon and the clouds, the grayest of whites mouthing formlessness like a yawn, diffusing the light (from where? somebody find out) demonstrate all the colors are at one's feet, a blue tarpaulin's puckered creases (the same as in inexhaustible clarity) cradling a little snow, while the pastel and green and blue of two houses and a garage drain the alley. White space gives way again to the objects on which the light sits, a humanity of provenance mucking about while the solecism demands a few links of snow to flit there as if rising. What happens next, the soundless rise of mayflies from the grass, as if someone has stepped in ash. The new world approaches. A kid holds a huge rope (incredible: the slowness of doors swinging closed against an accelerating current) while the walls in the lock grow shorter in the mechanical springtime, *canal de l'Ourcq*, cracking the spiral. Gate open, rope drawn in, the barge and the man in the street (it's me), freed of their chosen paces, play shadows, side-by-side until one of the low bridges forces the kid to crouch and the man to cross over. The barge slips below my feet and I feel the city underwater, squinting at the sunlight like a fish the cloud-like hull has just darkened. The promenade had become an endless waiting and the pause for catching up the simple lust. Hidden behind a tree no wider than my spine pressed against it, I'd never seen more of the bowl the surface of the Earth forms around an acceding presence, the world of objects narrowed to a pole, the zone expanding, and the imagined eyes, of the child calling me back. How strange and then lovely to be enclosed in what's called the feeling of escape, back in the old world again, coming upon the corner of a massive building in the street, fearful at first blink of cutting one's cheek on the vertical steel and glass that, as the eye again opens, soften into the streets and lakes that form its reverberating countenance, reflecting clouds, sky, and facades, touched in that way for the first time, as the tall rock in the middle of a wood holds the walker who (essential relative clause!) remains lost aloft in the canopy's lowest reaches, o intricate skeletons of light and shadow!

These people, that tower they came out of, shedding its darkness — a centrality was seen to move, like clouds across the moon when no wind is felt, or an accompaniment to which no one played or sang. I'd love to know what you, upstairs all day, were doing at that moment, low water at the beach, a sail behind the breakwater not touching anything else, and two girls with long shadows in a fantastically wide and shallow puddle, wider and shallower ("while it hailed in the orchard it rained in the village") than anything so temporary had ever seemed. When the water failed to deepen, we lowered ourselves full length. Later I changed my shorts below a towel and a man watched. A pause in the effort to clear a space had again become the space, as hesitation moved the runner onto the sand, and the phenomena of phenomena seen a thousand times was again being followed by the familiarity of an always newer (renewed) sensation: how unlike the familiar events all days are, except this one.

The sight of wind in the trees with sunlight and the sound of skateboards
and a boy's impression of an aria. Embarrassment in the presence of
a child. We thought we saw something real in the description of the
landscape in the irregular wheels on irregular asphalt, but it vanished
suddenly, having been loud consistently. That it often leaves in this
sudden manner does not clarify the relationship. The pigeons have their
own vortex, but for each one, or flock, depending on how many are
particular to the windrows of the buildings, the intersection, the spikes
in the station, to clothe the problem in its historical costume, and the
statues, a pair on horseback or one divided, from each of whose upraised
hand the spear has been thrown, though it looks stolen, and was, despite
the affect, sculpted missing.

Only no one wants to follow the example. The story-cut grass. The roar of an airplane. The hail on the embankment looked white, but not moving it between the tree and the grate it was gray and individual. As Hopkins writes, We have other such afternoons, one today. Like a string that had been bound around a blade, lifting us in and out of place, though now the shape it holds is there, where we had only been, and in the motion of the string remain, divided like the homophones *fait* and *fête*, imaginary feet held by force and beauty. By then the hail, like those outriders, had melted. The spirit of the age who has no trouble hearing the bombs in the stars while the teacher is excluded from the current life of objects, the kids draw the Maypole that fell on the stage at the potluck. A bill can't be lifted from the straight white streak, as Hopkins says elsewhere of those very same birds.

Supreme circumstance before last, supreme circumstance after next. One pink button in low-water mud and the fly on the window climbs the pine tree, drops glistening on the newly planted flowers. An apparent proximity. When part of his tooth broke off, he couldn't stop touching the space. But there is more to it than objects, as for instance weeding or not taking out the trash. And when the sun looked in, I shuddered at a singularity; everything was limited to the nausea of watching a blue jay in the rhododendron till it moved. The left wing lifted and didn't come down while the head was tightening the vertical. A peak is not a mountain, *mes amis*. Some precious *and* inhabits when you leave.

But how — A rainbow,
one of those — He
wanted to — And in
the little meadow —
The airplane had been
— The preceptor
captivates — The tree
goes

But how he admired her persistence, the drops filling the cistern over
an imponderable time, like writing out the letters in a book or thinking
(without weightlessness or nausea) of the pulse extending in both
directions like a two-headed string, without diplomacy or revenge, living
on as an actual man (a woman) in his (her) idea, namely the relation he
thought he had initiated between the two bodies and everything else he
thought to flee, like these sentences he'd written as her words' (that he still
couldn't chorus) late evening shadows.

A rainbow, one of those images of a limit, a horizon, an eyebrow, that holds its own by negating the desire to move even more, even the white gulls flying in the light between the eye and the rainbow don't move any more than a white line drawn across a blue paper can be said to move even as the rest of the afternoon is imagining without any effort (so much is it contained already in the line itself) the brush and the hand moving between the artist and the paper; a rainbow in two chunks above the lake, separated by clouds which one does not imagine whole as one imagines the rainbow whole or the book one reads from a friend's coffee table to be the right book or the bolts from the hardware store to fit the table or the narrow strip between the buildings to be larger than the whole, in which the only rainbow that can be written is the rainbow, the only fish the silver fish in the mouth of the gull flashing brighter, the only child the accidental unrelated child, the only wife a definite article in other words, like the color black or the green leaves of trees, the old bow-and-arrow TV antennas, which continues on all sides to accumulate the ants, the birds, the ivy, the crumbs, the drops of water on the leaves, the bird arriving at the eave, the sill. The will is everything if you are still as water through the window screen that only seems to break it up reminding me of the digital effect called *art* in which things seem to move by blinking on and off or in and out, as a way of making me wonder in which state it has coalesced, as there is a point at which coal cedes to the rainbow to the oil of the biofuel body in the sun, the very sun that no more erased than created the rainbow, the crumbling of an empire that had already, hundreds of years before, been heard.

He wanted to say something about her narrative. Someone else told it. After a brief contact (the small, scratchy flowers were open or known as waves) in which she was absorbed, it returned to the surface. The grass, shed by someone's boots, now bunched below the chair leg always a little shorter than the others, the one the toe of her foot kept touching, after all those years as a figment instead proved a past existence, a terror sunk in, obscured, absorbed by having been true always, having been drained of its ink by constant use, the work needs roof — she stumbled here and in the presence of her being carried upstairs it continued; speech and feeling alternated in the place by the fire and the low, dark undercurrent, just as the people, dead and living did. The strongest variable remained, scratched deeply into the wood, as if movements were comprised of frames, the lurching song of auto-tune, plotless novels built of scenes, the narrow roads wearing whatever wouldn't fit in the case I dragged behind; and sudden, explosive showers, here or there, sometimes twice a day, transformed the field (a lake of raspberry canes, a network of tiny, fractal ravines in the newly planted tomatoes) and the body (light and smooth, one emerges from the sea, the showerstall or storm, and the street also shines, body geared perfectly to the dazzling, continuous rail); but the figures at a burial appeared too, and the perfect incoherence of *Les Paysans*, though these last were ghosts mechanically returning the wobble to its roots, by exposing and seeming to tear them up, cut them out, and paste them down. I was reminded of a job I dreamed one night under my first position, in the earliest days of our confidence, I told her the lurching minutes (one is of the song) flow so quickly, riffled by the official, water-marked pages offered on the side of a mountain, that kind of book one is forbidden to write in, a prelude to things (here someone glanced into the fire) not yet completely in the past.

And in the little meadow, the one Ponge describes in *le pré*, there was a fire that was meant to trigger an imaginary bomb and succeeded, despite the lies we tell ourselves about where ideas come from. It was like those cases, intellectual and personal, in which suddenly it was the other identical (no, fraternal!) twin that one was in love with walking up an icy stream until boots had filled with water or feeling less than alone in the great ideas. A dying bird was meant, she found out later at the club, to be in flight when it was "taken." Next century. The wasps crawl in and out of the grapes that receive the hail most violently, and that image of violent reception, already doubled by the vivid prick of the thistle in the carpet, was meant to be the place taken away from yourself, the thick glass air edge of the cliff I peered over without knowing which side I was on.

The last summer had ended that way, too, and the economic vegetation, a bloody treadmill among the instincts to work yourself to death at its command, was finally also among those things that needed awakening from. But by then one was shucking corn, getting closer and closer to the indigestible kernel. It wasn't the idea at its essence that mattered (that was eternal and one continually outlasted it) nor the thing given rise to — that it had been these things, and would be them, and would never again thus be felt — but the act in which it was encountered, the child spinning (for the first time) deliriously against his will, above the parable of honey bees and clover.

The airplane had been higher than the moon and she had held her
hand higher than an imaginary sun. If the city were made of grammar,
I could find my way around, she added, but given the freedom with
which we've traded names and positions, poked around in the crevices
where we'd snuck away to be found hiding, choosing the exact spot the
seeker had chosen and crouching there with excitement, the gawww of
pronunciation, arms extending the air into buzzing without bees or hive.
Sewing yesterday and again today her frayed cuffs show something like
a gauze bandage where the cloth has worn away. The under fabric gives
shape, and the question, What's below that? I am looking at my shirt to
count the parts and stitches. I have a train ticket in my pocket I lost in
the pocket of a jacket I didn't wear all winter. I found the ticket on the
spring day I lost the jacket, having left it in a theater. In another pocket
of the lost jacket remain the sunglasses someone left in the rental car in
California. By then I'd transferred the ticket and the sounds of the house
in the bathtub to the city. A poem is painful for its truth content, no one
is around but the people in it, and the sidewalk's torn up sections, leaf-
printed sand and gravel, reveal that most inescapable of features, a new
surface.

The preceptor captivates me: Not everyone responds in the same way to these things, and, Perhaps everyone needs 3 or 5 minutes to speak her piece. She described to me the strange sensation one has during the 500th performance of a play and how difficult it is to explain there and then one's awe and giddiness to those companions speaking and acting freely from their own inclinations and who would deny, good-humoredly, a play was in progress. The spark from the overhead train competed at that moment with the dim stars and overcame them as we passed under the tracks. Are you going somewhere? I said to my companions. They smiled and I said again, Where are you going? At which the three of them, while we waited for the light to change from yellow to red and back to green again, went into hysterics, for though we were all on our way to the theater (I had simply exchanged its location in my mind with that of another theater, on the same street but further down and on the opposite side, an error for which I have a strong affinity) they had assumed, as so often before, that though we were travelling to the same place, all together, for the same performance and, even more comical to them, travelling at my behest and direction, that I thought we were still in the room, and even should be, a room now witness to the collision of stars near and far, trains and traffic signals, a room with several theaters between which to choose or, as it were, a room with several theaters between which to be so comically confused, a room from which the three of them were so casually departing, without the slightest word of explanation. This alone is the preceptor's story.

The tree goes down, then space goes up. Form is practice. I went out in my blue jacket, bumped the storm door with my asses. I was the neighbor. When he looked right, he was afraid of space from the deathless no-place of the OK solid object. Interrogation: I crossed a border once, but by then it had shifted and I felt included despite my best efforts in the single letter alphabet. Live for today, live for tomorrow! A series of idylls was what it felt more like, the sun in the blackness of the darkness of the giant's hand swinging like a lantern from September to June. The widow's walk on the gigantic captain's new house was trying to die a 19th century death, but the sea had changed too much, into a view from the eternity-disorienting heights of fabricated space. A bird sang in a clock. We set a place for the uninvited guest.

I saw — I already knew what — The unity paradox — Tried once to open — How small the connections — Often the upper body — The telescope — A near full moon

I saw you and then the elevator door opened and I saw you again for the first time. A self-portrait escapes like a cloud of sperm under Roman hot springs or a milkweed pod left open on the counter. I turned my back on the sun and the sun went behind a cloud. I predated the present troubles. I refused to speak in a crisis and gave out soft lips and a tightness between ears and nose. It was important to leave maple leaves, snow, an amorous viburnum at the edge of the woods where trees had been cleared and the new growth, opposite, simple and entire, took the shape of the graded land. A car turning left met spiders deep in the Queen Anne's Lace. There was a new iceberg visible from next summer's cottage and huge bells of fresh bronze in the church tower. Storms and calms chronicled. Responsibilities, long hours, carefree days sketched the ordeal of submitting to them. There was an obscure signature on the door of the office and at the bus stop someone stretched out in the grass claimed the gingko's leaves weren't ready to chew or apply to a wound. They were brown at the edges while the people who were waiting to board the bus and the people taking shelter were differentiated. At mid-morning, the sky still dark and the promised something big hadn't arrived. Days had been cancelled — which ones weren't clear. Along the stagnant pools separated by little pathways yellow flowers on long hairy stems had survived a handful of frosts. The pressure to go on living remained intense.

I already knew what it was going to look like, a decadent cycle, of growth and decay, that hadn't inspired confidence so much as substitute the world for the self in a pseudo-Heraclitian geometry coiled around a center dull and stony, pockmarked, inoculated against transference, and filled with other people waiting to get out who never would. And the brisk air fell before I could, promising survival, the gestural lines on the half-paved street, themselves soon to be covered with another layer, but followed in the blindness of good vision and as embarrassing (in the sense of revealing) as picture postcards elaborately framed to let two serigraphed lemons burgeon with the abeyance of message. So the singer doesn't know his song and the newcomers just back from the front are asking: what will be the new mode of fighting? We congratulate them on the shadows that reach back to the place they have deserted. It's a version of the future, the green and yellow ailanthus, heavy with winged fruit and dense flower clusters, where one is happy as long as exploring in the neighborhood, choosing between the statements: beneath an apparent unity, a thousand dissident styles; beneath an apparent dissidence, a thousand unitary styles. Rain runs off a low building, slanting roof hidden behind the purest cement parapet, a glorious feeling, and a parking sign is dragged down the sidewalk by a group of kids, to be one of many in the reader's huge, foreshadowed hand.

The unity paradox twists (is distorted) into relationship, bee slips into harbor, ship bumbles into flower — That promise of happiness, derived from catastrophe! — a crate of plastic watches, really toy insects, flashes in the total dark of the hold like lightning in the open field, then the fireflies of more than one becoming form, as if the long adherence to the image hadn't swallowed all processes, python-style, in the single agony of the disarticulated moment. It's all inversion, I wrote L, the inversion of the idea the reader thinks the reader is having, thinks the reader has had, and the delay of the inversion until it's read again, as a sentence, instead of a series of niches for the images, niches made of commas, or subordinate clauses, when it's all essential and relative. The idea before it's inverted is the idea of old arrangement, the old arrangement of the images that came to seem to be the images themselves, the succubus that is just a woman, the heavy perfume of the rose, the gutter running with lead that is the golden center, where one's exclusion is the marginalization of the object by the flow, where the subject lives, scrap of paper or disobedient turd kicked there by the green plastic of the broom, straight from the plastic straw factory floor, straw that never grows old even as it breaks down, those elements out of which I've composed my mannequin to the human as you have pulled the thread, I wrote L, unstitching the knot-letters, to leave once again the doubled thing, the thing itself, or themselves. With sunglasses on the house was blue on blue, as he said it had been against the brilliant white of snow, not its own white on its own blue as it had seemed before, as were the curtain, painting and comforter in the room, and the eyes of the child who expected someone else here where I was writing to you, I wrote L, *I* written *L*, the feeling of waking up having gone to sleep alone and finding, panicked and confused, that there was no one else there, as one shouldn't have been, had no reason to be, like one's hand on one's knee or one's hand conducting the words in the air without having been put there. *This is* not *really that*, and in fact the rose-stitched quilt twisted into an S taught me soundly how to sleep without the mistake, without which it still clicked, the *L* set the tip of the tongue against the roof of the mouth, but left the sides open for the free escape of the intonated breath. It had the feeling of being the same, though it wasn't the same at all. The true charm of a person escaped in the emptiest and most human intonation! which for poetry also is enormously important.

Tried once to open the door and go out into the street, under a puffy sky, before the millions of leaves of the elm. It was amazing and possible to see one, near the center, fluttering, compounded, a fever we'd sometimes mistaken for the various. What was being drained as we accumulated? The great hope when the daybook opened for a change of plans that would destroy that category was the result of not being phased in properly, of fully existing at times in spaces that contained levels, coffee dumped into a cup, leaves and sticks arranged on a stump, votes cast for what wasn't there at the moment of casting. We shifted, the city under the snow melted, and then in the spring tattered pink and white bills hung in the block's trees, flailed under windshield wipers, were riffled on doorknobs by the breeze, the body on the gibbet-mast, and hid in hands placed on sacrums and nodal feet, against lumps in the park that would never melt, between the edge of the bed and the sidewalk and the wall. The mutability on which we'd meant to love conquered with a process dark and cold, fusing the division we had meant to choose. When was it she had dug into the rotten shell of the English walnut with a powerful thumb and turned them both green? A laundry basket struggled down the street in the arms of a man. The bark of an elm on bare skin was smooth from these distances. It wasn't enough any more to say we felt diminished.

How small the connections! How large the content! To construct it any other way would be a new effort. Uniqueness, after all, follows from the intensity of the encounter, setting the dead leaf on the wheel that the foot has started spinning, feeling the little bumps on the skin.

A dream: up close, the fish larger and grayer than the storm. In a corner of the eye, a rabbit eats a blade of grass, one of the last, and the dead leaves bristle in the breeze off the canal. A feeling and a knowledge contest stupidity and the fact of its absence.

The blocks of town houses where we drop Louis Bardales, oriented toward their doubles on dead courts wedged between the sunken interstate and the D.O.T. warehouse composed of glass brick and fans ten times the size of the largest prop plane's propeller, can't be said to face inward any more than can the heart, lungs, liver, or kidneys, and Louis Bardales walking to his Aunt's in the target of multiple streetlights, pivots violently, trying to turn on those ghouls and shadows.

Often the upper body twists from the line of flight toward the dumpster, in whose jumble a few regular lines suggest an object, and then it stumbles the fairytale stumble of the lost child that leads to a cave or cottage barely delineated from the briars, a hidden desire, momentum overtaken by a deeper *raptus*, a business in the trenches between things, subconscious and material. And it was nothing; in this case a broken swing I easily resisted, though neither did I feel any shame — this was not, after all, a fairytale — when a friend came flying around the corner and into my arms, as if she were the plot attacking my story. It had the form of that happiness by which we recognize our madness — a chance encounter and a small divagation, magical devices — and we put it on vengefully, welcoming the mountainous reply of the buildings, in this narrow place, to our emphatical greetings. Then we dodged one of the decrepit pick-up trucks so weighed down with its load of metals — old aluminum 33 cents/pound, no. 1 heavy copper .99 — a trail of sparks was strewn behind it at the speed bump, though only to be devoured by snow and sun. In the truck's occupants — as experience had led me to expect, they seemed only half-asleep, waiting to catch their eyes in the pact of seeing, like sleepwalkers that do a great many things in their sleep which they would not dare or wish to awake — I saw the leaders of the secret public of the sovereign alleys, whom we greeted with a friendly nod, as with the same we had been identified as what we all were, the minds of other things, accidental cause of joy.

The telescope works. I saw the leaves on the tree across the street, the maple leaves caught up in the telephone wires, as if they were too large and close to be my leaves and my wires. The texture, of veins, and between the veins, individual cells, put us in another world entirely. An actor is unable to hold onto sunglasses or an umbrella. One dead man can play the other in the non-actor's life story. A book makes me think of a campground in Sicily, a few cabins and a few more tents under umbrella pines growing from the sand between a crumbling cliff and the sea in the perfect degree of sunlight, inside that hot, but not intolerably hot, day, through the needles to the sand and also from the bright sea and from the strip of sand where the trees had ended but the sea had not begun. Much earlier, years and years, I'd gotten drunk one New Year's Eve on sweet wine and, as I tried to swing myself onto the lowest branch of the huge oak in the center of a meadow where all the others from the party sat, I fell repeatedly onto the frozen ground. When I finally made it onto the dark branch and still could only hear voices and not see figures, I stopped laughing in the moment of feeling, even as it ended, at peace. Earlier, near midnight, I'd kissed everyone (disgusting everyone, a companion told me the next day, though a friend assured, again years later, that it wasn't the case). I'd also crawled around in the snow, unable to stand up "so slippery was the icy ground," instead moving quickly as a possum on my hands and knees. Such occasions stand out as times when independent action included fellowship, the secret to so many things which have since remained elusive.

A near full moon, the hunters' gibbous, that waxed suddenly, not out
of the weeks but the hours, and gave birth to a succession of airplanes
approaching as dots (they didn't grow but came into focus, the surface
of the lights becoming spiked and plural), emerging from the partially
restored face with the triangular form that suggested, either as result or
explanation of all those Madonnas with Child, a placid stability before
disappearing over the roof, reminding me I also know a man who leaves
me feverish (we meet rarely), staying present for days after, raging for a
greater understanding of the world *in toto* while pulsing (in his role as
medium the pulse — in one of spiritualism's familiar, discredited illusions
— is my own) like the wing lights of the planes, red and green, a singular
vitality that has the amazing (because so often such forces deaden in an
age of crudescent brightness) capacity to be newly recognized, exposing
and releasing in the old knowledge of our pleasures, powerlessness, and
complicity the gleam of a pearl that has been worried for years (cultivated,
as he himself has convinced me, as all — more amazing still their lustre
— pearls are, including those recovered by the poor fisherman's wife,
whose own worried dreams are to the same shocking degree knowable, or
those of the divorced oysterman, the other twin, who finds the occasional
— having left his days as a fishmonger behind — pearl in the oysters he
farms in the bay, finding, as it were, those pearls against his intentions,
the kind we await most self-consciously) which I am often imagining (an
attitude to knowledge he has used to convict me) but never hope (desire,
too, has a shell) to possess. Screams from the alley, the chain link fence
jangles, the power of the ball and foot, what does it mean to be convinced
of what one has experienced? Rhythm and beauty are spaced by the
tower, but I see it in the night sky's points and drones, an angle of sight
that brings things later and later to the ear, until finally it reappears in the
index under *erotic contact, architecture of.*

I am happy to be living
— The portable
doorbell — A boy
dropped — Long
sentences — 4:31 all
the bells rang

I am happy to be living in the age of ibuprofen, pain pills in general, the leaves of the ivy are at 6 different stages, glass or brick, the three directions, and looking and guessing, and exposure, tight pink buds diagramming the north glass and full-size leaves shading the southern brick. The line break is a technique equal to any other. The vault of heaven is a line break even for those inside it, the dome, the period when the dome was lost and just existed, the donkeys and livestock and vendors and keepers wandering the Pantheon in a rainstorm in orbit around the oculus, but the Panthéon keeps surfacing in Paris below the pulsing dome of the ring roads by which we were extended and missed our planes and exited the city in a rainstorm for the dome of sunlight of the south by way of the labyrinth, but not the one visible from Vaux-le-Vicente's creaking attic. We were at its drifting center in the city people live; the edge can be as absent as the rhyme in the pure block of the whole imaginary as it doesn't move through space. "I" drifted and it kept arriving at the bedside, to find itself there, eyes covered and weeping, eyes wide and shining, eyes hooded and forgiving, the fiction of what can't end there, the three impossible to fix dimensions. I waited for a long sign, the man might say to the woman, but you never came. For weeks I glanced at the hulk on the horizon (a water crib from which the whole lake sometimes seemed to spring; it had a dreamy sweetness in relation to the rest of the landscape) and waited for it to drift; but the water goes in to return to the surface. I wasn't wrong, I didn't tell him accurately, I am not bored by novels, and the way you say it is the house and the walls, the house where no character is made to cross the room, the walls I feel receding at my approach.

The portable doorbell from the old, evicted, sold, condemned, demolished apartment between the mystery of not wanting something actively and then being led to wanting it but not thinking of that as wanting it, a false step, as it felt, followed by a perfectly natural one that is nevertheless its result. Then what have you done. Then what. Then the color of the mind is an object, the hard tongue, a poem, probably the insidious feeling — of art, of friendship — inside a false structure, coupled to a genuine sensation, and the insidious attraction of the launched feeling, the structure falling away like the huge scaffolding beside the Apollo rockets in the early mornings of their childhood during the moon launchings, no longer needed except to fall away, followed by the falling away of the sections, and the feeling by exceeding it seeming to have escaped it, the capsule at the velocity called escape velocity, to which to feel we owe everything. Then the pain of a pin, a needle really, in the hard scar tissue softened it and released its pull on the fascia, which in turn released its pressure on the muscle, which in turn ceased over-stimulus of the afferent nerve's free endings, which in turn ceased their excessive transmitting of second messengers through the dorsal horn directly to the thalamus or indirectly to the frontal cortex for further processing, which in turn fell silent, which in turn lay dormant, though only after the shock that lifted the whole sequence so far out of non-being it had far enough to fall to generate velocity sufficient to fall back more deeply into it.

A woman buys a loaf of bread and skip-runs across the street with it and into the green and red door. She is one thing you are certain not to draw in response to this.

There is also something natural about the potatoes and oranges and bananas at the greengrocer's.

Instead a lecture about whether or not to rinse the dishes before stacking them in the sink. The river and the lake just visible through the trees. The clothes hung on lines in the yellow room so that the outer world seems to be inside this inner world and so that this inner world seems to be inside the outer world and so this inner world seems to be an inner world and so that outer world seems to be an outer world and so there seem to be inner and outer worlds.

A boy dropped a wrapper to the ground. His friend was in short sleeves, two t-shirts. It skated above the sidewalk like a waterbug before settling. The icicles from the wave-spray had gotten longer, some had broken when they touched the surface. They were heavy now and no longer looked like the fringe of beads on a necklace. I had started hearing a voice and then I wanted to see things and by writing them down let it talk, and not the reverse. And when the voice changed, as it has, that didn't. The leaves fell off the trees. The po-lice are going to come by and arrest them. The radiators are so hot I have opened the window. Help yourself bitch, and much laughter. The sun is just above the building across the street. The sun is not solid. A form of cirrus twisted by winds. The laboring sea goes up into the capitol C, a meaning forced upon it by the climb, and so a blood spot slow again. The dreads were real, the air much softer than it had been before. The finches on the wire watched the people overlapping. O we went down more than he went up. Empty the tax preparer's office and offices of Southern Manufactured Homes. We left the empty office for the sun before it went behind the building, for the laboring sea and then the finches overlapping on the wire and the people inside the landing of condos boarded up against the one we saw climbing out, having long since established residence behind the barrier. And then the whistle of the train, a promise of the earlier whistle, a large cluster of anthills. Two kids in the condos on the balcony above the sea undertook the sex thing. The letters appeared larger, staying after. The sun went on and on toward the building. We were a little rebuffed, as if this wasn't happening to us. A car with a tiny camera on the roof spun its wheels in the gravel. Rebuffed, overlapping, the great cliff of the façade of the abandoned condos' upper floors rose to chase us when we ran away, stopping when we stopped, continuing again, as it must here, a series of waves more than a dream. But when we turned the corner there it stayed, with the illegal ones balanced on the cliff, the immigrants and kids.

Long sentences for when little is happening, short for when much goes on. A new moon. Kids smoking with a perfect view of it and the sun setting, though most have their backs turned. Now I know where that happens, across from the lower boulangerie and the *Bar / Presse / Tabac*, where the village ends against the field. A woman with a small child has just left them. She's saying *bon soir* and laughing. Though they are behind a low wall and under an olive tree I guess it's not a secret. When one inhales, I can see their faces in the glow of the cigarette. When another strikes a match, their faces turn white. I can see the faces of those with their backs to the sunset, the mountains' silhouette, the new moon. As strange as it may seem, the work interested me. The old men (they've gone home now) bend at the waist to pick up their *boules* (no squatting). But one has a rod with a magnet on the end. He's not bending when the others do, and he stands up straighter. A young man, taller than his friend, even after the friend steps up onto the curb, pauses to greet some others. Some he kisses and some, he takes their hands. Must one have opinions? His motorcycle boots have 6 buckles and his leather jacket comes to his knees. His head is shaved, but his beard and moustache are cut close. He catches up with me in the *bière* aisle (here the pronunciation hardly changes) and I retreat to the canned tomatoes for awhile. Four years before you didn't come to see the meteor shower, the Perseids, just said hello at 4 a.m. and went home. Like them, we're called by the place we come from, but that's not our origin. If those teenagers were a constellation, they'd be the shield of Perseus, and I'd have been looking into them to slay the Gorgon of the enthralling sunset. There isn't any instead. I adored them. The night before a lit cigarette came rolling down the cobblestones and I quickened my pace to step on it. The street was deserted, but not to the extent I'd imagined. In the end, it's possible. But I was on my way home to be fashioned by this dream into a new sensation, a few hours — they're everywhere, too — before the Perseids resumed.

4:31 all the bells rang the street washer advanced and the man put the sheets back in the trash but took the blanket with the red border. The angle irons painted white the bolts hold the window they don't make faces. A scream drew me to the other side of the table and when I looked out I was still typing on the far side seeing nothing. A boy takes a hand off his friend's shoulder to let the street sign pass between them. Hands with a ring and a gold watch pull up the toddler's blue pants. Only some of the white vans have *fuck you* graffiti. Please explain the function of churches, graffiti, statues of Jesus, cemeteries, money. James wants to know. And also whether or not we own the rooms we are renting all three and didn't he used to call any place we spent a night home. Money is the most important thing of all, says James. I dispute him but he says: we need money to love each other because if you didn't have any money I would get you something to eat. Buildings longer than they are tall, taller than they are long, buildings with an almost perfectly square façade are rare, but Paris on the whole is a square city, the rolling fields of the rooftops. I no longer want to say what many are doing.

A man runs down the sidewalk, cuts between a gap in the cars to the street, runs straight down the center of the street until a gap in the cars on the opposite side appears, then cuts sharply to the sidewalk and continues running. The pinwheel turns, the other pinwheel is gone. Two identically dressed children one has a red and white back-pack and the hats are off-white and pink and those shoes are red, the others olive-green. The railroad tracks a small waste ground moss on stone embankments a non-sidewalk of brambles the fluffy seeds of trees above a car-dealership. A pigeon flies down the street, and the train seems to have turned the corner, a young woman walking with her right hand over her left hand, unavoidable formulation. In *Brigadoon* Jeff at the crowded bar lights three cigarettes at once. At first we take this for a comic exaggeration of his anxiety. But then he orders two glasses of water and puts the extra cigarettes in ashtrays and slides them over, claiming the stools on either side of him. It's a little theater he's made in New York, complete with footlights.

Afterword

The distortion comes from assigning the flower or grain of sifted gravel in the road bed a single sensation, an integument of exposed nerve endings. The doll floated face-down in the stream, the cords of its body held up by the wooden hands, head, and feet. We watched from a window and out of the streaming water and the long weeds flowing in the indirect light a hand, without surfacing completely, turned the doll over to float face up. It was a kindness and we wondered how it was that the hand was coming (it was one of those actions, however brief, that seems continually to be happening and about to happen, probably as the wandering mind replays it) from below the surface and returning to the depths, when it ought to have been reaching down into the water and then returning to the air, close to where we were standing.

I identify the knocking as a lilac that has grown close enough to the house, the fort, the dollhouse (an architectural maquette or spot), the door of the fort slamming in the wind, the inhabitant sneezing as she rides up past the garbage truck on her bike. Things are connected by sounds, spaces and shapes, ideas, and plots, though sometimes there's a hand below the book when it closes, a decisive point, that feeling which one returns to the earth and radiates out of, reading the map's transit by sleeping and riding to the route ends (Stillwell, Kimball, or Porte d'Orléans), then disembarking, depleted but together, at the surfaces that we can hear, can smell.

Richard Meier is the author of two previous books of poetry, *Terrain Vague*, selected by Tomaž Šalamun for the Verse Prize, and *Shelley Gave Jane a Guitar*. He is writer-in-residence at Carthage College and lives in Madison and Chicago.

Photo Credit: Jane Williams

In the Pure Block of the Whole Imaginary
by Richard Meier

Cover text set in Chaparral Pro.
Interior text set in Adobe Jensen Pro.

Cover art by Jane Williams, photograph:
"East Boston, November 9, 2011"

Cover and interior design by Cassandra Smith

Omnidawn Publishing
Richmond, California
2012

Ken Keegan & Rusty Morrison, Co-Publishers & Senior Editors
Cassandra Smith, Poetry Editor & Book Designer
Gillian Hamel, Poetry Editor & OmniVerse Managing Editor
Sara Mumolo, Poetry Editor & OmniVerse New-Work Editor
Peter Burghardt, Poetry Editor & Bookstore Outreach Manager
Turner Canty, Poetry Editor & Features Writer
Jared Alford, Facebook Editor
Juliana Paslay, Bookstore Outreach & Features Writer
Craig Santos Perez, Media Consultant